MORE
than a
MARTIAL
ARTIST

THE STORY OF HOW
ONE MAN'S LIFE HAS
IMPACTED THE LIVES OF
MILLIONS...

Dr. John F. Williams

Elite
PUBLICATIONS

Publisher: Elite Publications, Greenville, NC 27858
Language: English
Paperback ISBN: 9781736833841
eBook ISBN: 9781736833858
Imprint: Elite Publications
Front/Back Cover and interior layout/design by: Tiger Shark, Inc.

Elite Publications, 1290 E Arlington Blvd, Greenville, NC 27858
http ://www.elitepublications.org

Ordering Information: Special discounts are available on quantity purchases by corporations, associations, educators, and others. For details, contact the publisher at the above address U.S. trade bookstores and wholesalers: Please contact Jessie Bowen. Tel: (919) 618-8075 or email info@elitepublications.org

PRINTED IN THE UNITED STATES OF AMERICA

"Martial Arts is like a mountain top...you see the top, and you hike and hike, and you climb up, and you finally reach the peak. But then you realize it was a false summit, but in front of you lies an entire new mountain range!"

-Dr. John F. Williams

Table of Contents

Foreword

Often, we see others with unique gifts and wonder why they are not using them to help themselves and others. When I saw that my sweet wife had a special gift for writing, I encouraged her to write her book. I wanted to dedicate this book to my wife, Dr. Brenda Lee Williams, and my children, Trevon Fitzgerald Williams and my daughter, Brejon Lana Reed, and my adopted son, Malaki Fitzgerald Williams.

These are the people that on earth keep my heart beating. I know that sometimes they probably thought I was the worst, but we may have thought that about all of our parents when we all look back. I praise God for allowing me to have a super son-in-law, Timmon Reed, who loves my daughter and the two children they have.

Thank God for our eight grandchildren because they mean the world to us, as they play a big part in keeping us young. This is what being more than a martial artist is all about. I am sending many blessings here today, thanking God for yet another day that was NOT promised to us.

I send special thanks to my pastor and first lady—Bishop Wilbur D. Vincent, as well as the 1st Lady Suganah Vincent. And my Center of Faith Church of God and Christ Church family Thank you for your blessings through God's word. You have, through Jesus, made me a better man.

One must remember that "You've got to find what you love and the only way to be truly satisfied is to do what you believe is great work. And the only way to do great work is to love what you do. So, if you haven't found it yet, keep looking.

Don't settle. As with all matters of the heart, you'll know when you find it. I've found that this journey has been incredibly freeing. Because no matter what happened, I had the peace of mind knowing that all the chatter, the name-calling, the doubting, all of it was just noise.

It did not define me, it didn't change who I was, and, most importantly, it couldn't hold me back. "This will be my first full-length book. "I was completely unprepared, but my lack of awareness of my limitations masqueraded as confidence, propelling me into the Who's Who of Martial Arts, a couple of Hall of Fames, four Doctor's degrees, and a black man who owns his own company!

I had to figure it all out, and my belief that I could handle these things, contrary to all evidence of my ability to do so, was half the battle. I WAS that black man that couldn't read and write, failed three times in the 7th grade, was always told what I couldn't and wouldn't be.

But, as I stand before you today, I can honestly say that I look back on MY life and start to second-guess myself. I can honestly say that I am a testimony, not just a witness! What I have discovered is this: You can't do it alone. Listen. Say 'yes.' Live in the moment. Make sure you play with people who have your back.

This is your time, and it feels normal to you, but really, there is no normal. There's only change, and resistance to it, and then more change. You must go through life with more than just a passion for change; you need a strategy. I'll repeat that. I want you to have passion, but you must have a strategy. Not just awareness, but action. Not just hashtags, Real Work, Real Work about REAL CHANGE!

Learn from every mistake because every experience, encounter, and particularly your mistakes are there to teach you and force you into being more who you are. And then figure out what the next right move is. And the key to life is to develop an internal moral, emotional G.P.S. that can tell you which way to go.

Everything comes to an end. But everything always begins, too. The fireworks begin today. Always be a first-rate version of yourself, instead of a second-rate version of somebody else. Stop being afraid of who is watching you. Give them something POSTIVE for them to watch! You may never know what results will come from your actions, but if you do nothing, there will be no result.

What lies behind us and what lies before us are tiny matters compared to what lies within us. No, no, no, the sky is not the limit. It is only the beginning. Never bend your head. Always hold it high, look the world right in the eye, and know that it takes courage to grow up and become who you are and, just remember, you can't climb the ladder of success with your hands in your pockets.

So, listen. Surround yourself with doers. Be around people who demonstrate their boldness. If you haven't found it yet, keep looking. Don't settle. As with all matters of the heart, you'll know it when you find it. My wish for you is that this life becomes everything that you desire it to be. So your dreams stay big, your worries stay small, and you never need to carry more than you can hold!

You may not always have a comfortable life, and you may not always be able to solve all of the world's problems at once. Still, history has shown us that courage can be contagious, and hope can take on a life of its own, which is why I can genuinely say that I am more than a Martial Artist!

-Dr. John Fitzgerald Williams

Dedication

To My Father and Mother, Mack "Forklift" Williams and
Arie Lee "Peaches" Williams.

Thank you, Mackie Lee Varnado, for being a huge part of my
upbringing. I owe you much love.

In Loving Memory

You are gone but not forgotten...

Willie Mae Walker

Maybell Bates

Mack Williams

Lawanna K. Rogers

Arie Lee Bates

Oscar Robinson

Charles Robinson

James Lee Williams

Sylvester Joe Williams

Mary Ann Blair

T.W. Taylor

June Taylor

Dondeagio Bennett

...And All Other Family Members and Friends!

My Wife, My Queen

This may seem like something out of the fairy tale book, but I remember the first time I met my wife. Brenda Lee (Payton) Williams, we had both just broken up with the persons that we were dating and me being in college in New Mexico and with her just getting out of High School.

I arrived in California from Eastern New Mexico University College during spring break. I just knew that she was the one when I saw a PICTURE of her. We met on a Wednesday, and I asked her to marry me on a Saturday, and it has been 33 years later.

This woman has been my everything, and one must understand

that every day will not be Sunday but understand Monday is the next day. So, what I tell everyone that takes the time to listen is that you must continue to do what it took to get him or her.

Never think that you have that person just because you are married. You must also love yourself and be in a good place with yourself before you try to join in matrimony with someone else.

That comes from a man who has been married for 33 plus years and has served in the military. Remember what you did to get them!

FRESH ANOINTING CHRISTIAN BIBLE INSTITUTE

Dr. Alice L. Basnight

II Corinthians 5:21 (KJV)

For he hath made him to be sin for us, who knew no sin; that we might be made the righteousness of God in him.

"It is up to me if it is to be.
You may mourn your old habits, but your goal will always
remain the same."

Dr. Oh God Angela Harris

What Are You Being Judged On?

Judge not, and ye shall not be judged: condemn not, and ye shall not be condemned: forgive, and ye shall be forgiven. Luke 6:37

We all fall prey to a powerful yet subtle temptation from time to time: the temptation to judge others. We judge them based on the lineage of the school they attended, rather than their size, the way they speak, or the martial arts school they attended. Yet, there are many times that we should just be thankful that we can still do what we do. You see, the way you think and feel about yourself, including your beliefs and expectations about what is possible for you, determines everything that happens to you.

When you change the quality of your thinking, you change the quality of your life, sometimes instantly. Just as positive words can make someone smile or a well-timed humorous quote can make someone laugh, our thoughts react to the world in real-time.

You have complete control over only one thing in the universe and that is your thinking. It's time to stop judging each other and start working together to make each other better, one kick at a time. As a white belt, I used to admire the dedication of the higher-level belts. I watched their forms with great intensity, as well as their actions. I understand that empathy, imagination, hard work, and many late nights go into your success, as they do in every great martial art and every successful individual.

Many say that they are inspiring leaders and want to make a difference in their schools and communities by seeking opportunities to serve others. This can be as simple as reading to a younger child or helping a classmate with your favorite subject. It can involve working in a team, like starting or joining a club at school or serving food with other volunteers at a homeless shelter. This is not a luxury, nor is it judged; it is hard work because hard work matters. Telling your story through the individuals that have been placed in your life for such a long time, because your legacy deserves to be recognized and honored.

Worrying

Another kind of mental clutter that many people deal with involves worrying. For some people, this worrying can be chronic. While it is acceptable to worry about certain things every once in a while, when the worry starts to take over your life, it becomes chronic and can even become addictive or compulsive. For example, for those who worry excessively, it might be challenging for them to recognize that certain situations are out of their control.

Not everything in life is predictable, but for some people, this fact can sometimes prove to be unbearable for them.

This results in a cluttered, worried mind. Another reason why worrying can take up a lot of valuable mental space is that unpredictability means the future is uncertain.

Worrying is a prime example of the fact that anxieties beyond your control often cause mental clutter. However, by shifting the focus of your mind onto more positive aspects of life, it is possible to evade and eliminate a large portion of mental clutter that has built up.

Fear

Fear can also clutter your mind and prevent it from effectively processing information. If you have ever experienced the feeling of dread regarding a situation that you've never dealt with before, then you're aware of the fact that fear can stop you in your tracks.

Fear can prevent you from being able to accomplish what should or needs to be performed while also being able to manipulate your brain in the process.

If you allow fear to penetrate your mind to the point that it's preventing you from doing something to move you closer to your goals, then it should be clear that fear is an essential kind of mental clutter that you need to eliminate from your life.

Guilt

Guilt or shame typically manifests in the mind when we're not happy with the decisions that we've made that we aren't excited about. This becomes twofold when the choices that we've made in the past end up hurting people we care about or people who have trusted us somehow. Guilt can end up taking a lot of mental space up in your mind when you cannot let go of your poor choices.

Instead of letting these poor decisions go and allowing them to become a learning experience, people can sometimes cling to their feelings out of guilt, or even shame. This kind of clinging fuels a situation where the individual allows their self-worth to become tarnished and allows low self-esteem to develop. Additionally, guilt and shame can end up opening up your mind and letting negative self-talk through. For example, if you feel guilt or shame about a situation from your past, you can start to become resentful or angry toward yourself. Once you become angry and upset, negative thoughts can start to form and take hold of your mind.

Acknowledging feelings of guilt and shame is the first step toward relinquishing your mind from the grasp of responsibility. Once you can recognize these kinds of emotions in yourself, you can start to forgive yourself and form a more positive relationship with your mind.

Regret

The final kind of mental clutter is regret. It is essential to realize that every single, self-defined, happy person in this world has more than likely done something that they regret. Making a bad decision is just one of the unfortunate realities of being human. It is not about the decision itself, but rather it is more about how you deal with the decision when the outcome isn't what you expected. It's common for people to focus more on the result of a situation and less on what was learned from a single experience. Being human involves being able to objectively look at what went wrong and where you can improve. However, it is entirely possible to become caught up in the past rather than being optimistic about your future.

A common thread runs through these five types of mental clutter and can be best described as an inability to let go. If you identify with any of these kinds of mental clutter, the chances are high that you are sometimes too hard on yourself, which can block your ability to gain mental clarity. The ability to release yourself from the burden of knowing that you could have done something differently is essential if you want to find mental clarity.

Now that you know some of the most significant kinds of mental clutter that could be causing you to lose focus, you must understand some of the specific triggers that can lead to a more cluttered mind.

"Only thing that makes one happy is being happy with oneself."

-Taylor J.

The Real A'Cire

I had to rise above the odds in order for a stronger me to emerge!
"Emerging Beyond"
-A'Cire

The News

For many people, the daily news can be a trigger point that ends up causing unnecessary worry, guilt, and stress. These days, it can sometimes seem as if everything on the news focuses on violence, controversy, or negativity. If you are used to watching the nightly news, you can determine if it is a trigger point for you by keeping track of how you feel afterward.

Either write down how you feel, or you can use your phone to record your feelings. It's essential to note the emotions that might arise associated with the types of mental clutter discussed previously. Once you've registered your feelings after watching the nightly news, could you take a few nights off from watching it? Take a step back from the chaos and see how you feel. You may find that your mind is a bit clearer when you refrain from watching it.

While this doesn't mean that you should completely hide from current events around the world, by recognizing that the news can sometimes clutter your mind in unexpected ways, you might be able to protect it better when necessary.

Money

Another trigger point that may cause you mental clutter is the subject of money. It doesn't matter where you are regarding your career; money causes everyone a lot of fear, worry, and even regret. If you continuously think about money and how to get more of it, there are a few things that you can do to help you think about it less. Start by altering your mindset.

Rather than being anxious and worried about the lack of money you have, try being grateful for the money that you do have. Then you need to be upfront with yourself about where the money you do make is going. After you determine where you spend your money, you can start to cut costs wherever possible.

The Past

Sometimes the past is simply a reference point as we move through life. However, this doesn't mean that we should allow the past to define our future.

When you focus on the past, it can seem like your inner demons shine brighter than they should. We've all made mistakes, taken others for granted, and have done things that we are not proud of. When you focus on these negative aspects of your past rather than the positive ones, you are more likely to be overly hard on yourself.

If you can start to think of the past as being less defining to who you are today, it can lead to a less cluttered mind when you are making important decisions.

Your Current Habits

It is entirely natural to get stuck in your current ways, even if the circumstances don't make you particularly happy. However, if you feel as if you have an attitude that you can't change things because it's just how it is, then this is a great place to start decluttering your mind and gaining mental clarity.

Suppose you think that your current circumstances are causing a significant level of mental clutter, in your life. In that case, you should look at your associates, your material possessions, and your job to see if any of them need altering. Then make a plan to address these things to get rid of the mental clutter and gain more mental clarity and achieve greater success.

What Can You Change To Make A Life Better?

_____

_____

_____

_____

_____

_____

_____

_____

_____

_____

_____

_____

These Are The Things That I Am Most Thankful For!

_____

_____

_____

_____

_____

_____

_____

_____

_____

_____

_____

_____

_____

_____

_____

_____

_____

_____

And we know that all things work together for good to them that love God, to them who are the called according to his purpose. Romans 8:28 KJV.

"Keep your face to the sunshine and you cannot see a shadow." Don't' look back, you are not going in that direction. Once you replace negative thoughts with positives ones, you will start having positive thinking and a willing attitude will allow you to do everything better and enjoy the journey." -Demetra L. Warrior

When Times Get Hard These Are The Things That I Must Remember!

_____

_____

_____

_____

_____

_____

_____

_____

_____

_____

Food For Thought! #1

**Life is 10%what happens to you and 90% how you react
to it. Are you where you want to be in life right now?**

_____

_____

_____

_____

_____

_____

_____

_____

_____

_____

_____

Food For Thought! #2

In life, nothing can satisfy and please your soul as much as helping others. Not only helping the needy will make a difference in their life, but it would also have a lot of benefits for you as well.

_____

_____

_____

_____

_____

_____

_____

_____

The Power Of Positive Thinking

Positive thinking isn't merely about making you feel happier or providing you with a more optimistic outlook. While these two outcomes are by-products of thinking positively, there are far more benefits that can change your mental clarity and help you achieve greater success.

Recent studies have shown that positive thinking is directly linked to your brain's reward system and pleasure stimulus. This means that once your mind feels the pleasure that positive thinking or happiness brings, it will reward itself in the hope of receiving more of this type of feeling. Positive thinking can have a snowball effect on the brain, and once you start thinking positively, your brain isn't going to want you to stop. Instead, positive thinking will entice your mind to continue to think this way so that you feel good more often. The manifestations of being able to think more positively about your behavior regarding your interactions with people you encounter throughout your day will include being more optimistic.

The Brain and Optimistic Thoughts

From a more scientific perspective, positive thinking has been proven to influence the growth that takes place in the brain. Specifically, positive thinking has been linked to stimulating the growth of neural connections in the brain. Of course, even if you don't typically think positively, these connections will continue to grow, but they will grow faster when you think positively.

This is important because as you get older, your brain's ability to develop these connections will inevitably start to slow down. When you can begin to think positively, it means your mind will function more efficiently for a more extended period. Along with motivating the growth of neural connections in your brain, two other benefits that come with positive thinking are related to doing output and analysis. Thinking positively has been linked to bringing the mind to process thoughts more quickly and be more alert.

Along these same lines, it has also been linked with solving complex problems in less time more efficiently. For example, when your thoughts are negative, it can sometimes seem like we are only thinking of the poor outcome regarding a particular situation. However, when our thoughts are more optimistic, we are more likely to be open to experiencing various results. This allows our brains to think of broader scenarios when it comes to finding solutions to our problems.

You Are What You Think

Another way you can look at positive thinking regarding decluttering your mind is to recognize that our thoughts often lead us to action or inaction. However, for those who think positively, they can see the world as a better place, where there are more opportunities and where they can accomplish anything they desire.

On the other hand, negative thinking often leads people to believe that the world is where their current circumstances are the only circumstances that they will ever realize. While the positive thinkers use their positive thoughts as a platform to take a leap and strive to achieve their dreams, those who think negatively will use their negative thoughts to limit what they produce and ultimately stops them from growing. It would help if you remembered that everything is constantly in flux.

Take the time to understand that as a human, you are continually evolving. Therefore, settling and thinking negatively about your personal growth is something that you should avoid. This is why positive thinking is critical because people often become their thoughts.

How to Become More Positive

Now that you know why thinking positively is essential for your success, it's time to discover how you can become a more positive person. While some people seem to be born with a greater sense of positivity, it doesn't mean that it isn't something that you can learn yourself. The first thing that you need to understand is that optimistic people aren't always positive. These people fully understand that being too positive can also be detrimental to their health and mental clarity.

Instead, positive thinkers are typically those who see both the good and bad in any given situation. Yet, they choose to focus on the good instead of the bad. This is an excellent place to start when you want to try and be more optimistic.

It is essential that you fully understand that there is a difference between someone blindly optimistic to the point of harm and someone realistic about what could go wrong and what could go right. Finding this kind of balance is significant, especially if you tend to have more negative thoughts than positive thoughts.

Rather than going all out and trying to be as optimistic as possible, it would be better for you to learn how to recognize both the good and the bad in a particular situation before you consciously turn your focus on the positive aspects of the situation at hand.

Volunteer Your Time

When you can discern the difference between being blindly optimistic and being realistic, you can start to look at ways to become more positive. An excellent way to do this is through volunteerism. You can volunteer your time in a variety of ways.

Write Down What You're Grateful For

If volunteering your time in your community isn't something you enjoy, you can become more optimistic by keeping a gratitude journal. Every night before you go to bed or when you first wake up in the morning, spend some time writing down everything that you are grateful for in your life.

When you do this, you only want to think about the current day if you are doing this at night or the previous day if you choose to do this exercise in the morning. This will help train you to think more about the positive details in your life rather than the negative and will likely help you see that your life has many amazing aspects.

Be Kinder

A great way to shift your mindset from negative to positive is to be kinder to those around you. When you are trying to be more positive, you must create an environment where you are kinder to the people in your life. Not only will this allow you to see your world from a different perspective, but you will also start to reconsider how you live your life daily.

Learning how to think more positively isn't just an essential exercise for your sanity, but it can also help to improve your health. You have the power to change the way you think, and thinking positively can help you clear the clutter from your mind and gain more mental clarity so that you can enjoy greater success in your business.

What Is Life After Martial Arts Me?

"If size mattered, the elephant would be king of the jungle."

How Do You Measure Yourself?

_____

_____

_____

_____

_____

_____

_____

_____

_____

_____

_____

Food For Thought! #3

"Kata often begins and ends on the same spot. Isn't that the circle of life? Perhaps by taking the application of Kata seriously, one can find astonishing answers in life."

_____

_____

_____

_____

_____

_____

_____

_____

_____

_____

Food For Thought! #4

"Choose your battles wisely. After all, life isn't measured by how many times you stood up to fight. It's not winning battles that makes you happy, but it's how many times you turned away and chose to investigate a better direction. Life is too short to spend it on warring. Fight only the most, most, most important ones, let the rest go." - C. Joy Bell

_____

_____

_____

_____

_____

_____

_____

_____

_____

When I Look At My Former Students What Lesson Can I Learn?

Food For Thought #5

"If you set your goals ridiculously high and it's a failure, you will fail above everyone else's success." -James Cameron

_____

_____

_____

_____

_____

_____

_____

_____

_____

_____

Be Clear About Your Goals

If you want to achieve self-discipline, you must have a clear vision of what you want to accomplish. This is non-negotiable. Everything else is a non-starter.

You may have everything figured out, you may even have a solid game plan on how to go about doing things, but none of that matters if you don't have a clear vision of what you seek to accomplish.

Goals are Not Wishes

I can't even begin to tell you how many people think that they already have goals and plans in life. If you ask them for specific details, it turns out that they don't have goals. They have a clear idea of where they'd like to end up.

There's no shortage of people imagining themselves living in palatial homes, possessing big bank accounts, and driving a fine Italian sportscar. But these are not goals. Instead, these are fantasies and wishful thinking.

You know you have a goal when you can take that endpoint of you living in this castle and then explaining clearly to yourself the backward steps you need to take to get there. That's when you know you have goals.

A clear plan outlines each step you must take in order to reach your goals. The goals often line up to make larger goals, which produces other outcomes. And these then line up to create even bigger goals. So, for example, if you want to be a lawyer in California, generally speaking, you have to take the bar exam. For that to happen, generally speaking, you have to go to an accredited law school.

Well, the problem is, not just anybody can go to law school. Most of the time, you have to have a college degree or some sort of academic credential. So while it does happen that people who did not finish high school can become lawyers, they take a different route.

If you want to take the general route of becoming a lawyer, you have to get a 4-year degree. To get a 4-year degree, you have to apply to college. To apply to college, you have to take an entrance exam.

Do you see how this works? You have the grand goal for yourself, which is to become an attorney, but there are the sub-goals that you have to go through. You have to go on a journey. And with each victory lies another path that requires another victory. That's how life is, regardless of what endpoint you're looking at.

Your endpoint might be to find yourself in a grand mansion. Great. Awesome. But you have to pay attention to the series of goals that need to be achieved before you reach that endpoint.

Goals Require Prioritization

Once you have a clear idea of the steps you need to take to achieve your ultimate goal, the next step is to set your priorities straight. You may have a nicely laid out path to go from where you are to where you need to go. That is great.
The problem is, if you have other responsibilities, duties and obligations, it's very easy to get lost in the weeds.

It's very easy to think that your job, which doesn't lead to your goals, is your number one priority. So, you don't take classes. You drop semester after a semester because you're working on your job. The problem here is that your job isn't tied directly to your goal. Sure, your job produces money so you can afford to work on your ultimate goal, but that is the extent of its proper relationship to your goal. Do you see my point?

If you prioritize your job first, then your goal decreases in importance. And before you know it, it goes out of mind. It ceases to be essential and you remain stuck where you are.

The moment you decide on your ultimate vision for your life is the moment you must also choose to reprioritize your life.

As important as your job is to put food on the table, please understand that it's of secondary importance to the grand vision you are pursuing. Live your life accordingly. In none of this advice do I say that you drop your job. I'm not saying that at all. That's not what I'm encouraging you to do. Instead, put everything in proper focus and invest your energy accordingly.

The Great Thing About Crushing Goals

The most extraordinary thing about crushing goals is that you get a nice surge of energy and possibility once you clear one hurdle. For example, when somebody wants to become an attorney, they must first get into college. When they take the SAT and do well and get into a good college, it feels good. They built discipline there.

When you free up your energy, clearing that first hurdle of getting into a 4-year university, you have to redirect that to the next step: taking the LSAT and finishing college with high enough marks to get into a good school.

Once you're there, you need to do well in your first year to get an excellent job with a big law firm or a prestigious practitioner that will later open doors for your career. Everything is tied together. And that's why you have to be very careful of how you channel your energy as you clear one hurdle after another.

A lot of people confuse clearing a critical goal as an excuse to relax. No. Don't do it that way. That's a nonstarter.

To a certain extent, trying to achieve success by being self-disciplined is like being a shark. Did you know that if a shark isn't swimming, it's dying? The same goes with you. If you're not pushing forward to the next goal, you're stagnating. And before you know it, you're going to find yourself in a very tough spot.

Step by Step Guide to Proper Goal Identification

Step #1: Start your day with a list of tasks that you need to accomplish.

Knock out one task at a time. Don't get emotionally caught up in each task. Allow the energy and sense of relief released by completing one task to carry over to the next task.

Step #2: Visualize your grand goal.

Think of what you truly desire in your life. I'm talking about your big goals here.

Think about what it would feel like. Think about what you would look like when you are living that kind of life. Come back to this vision before you begin a daily task, and after you complete it. When you do this, you line up all the small, nitty things you're doing now to something bigger. This reminds your subconscious, as well as your conscious mind, that everything that you do now has meaning. Every step you take now will ultimately lead to the grand victory you are working so hard for.

Step #3: Write down your grand vision for yourself every day.

In the morning, write down your grand vision. Read it, visualize it, and then crumple the paper. And then, starting with a fresh page of paper, write it down again.

When you do this, you refresh your subconscious and your conscious mind. You also filter out visions and goals that are not really all that important. Maybe you think that you're supposed to go after them because other people desire them. But if you refresh your life's grand vision this way, a lot of that extra stuff falls out. What's left are the things that are truly important in your life. These are the goals that stick. These are the things that you know, deep down inside, will always remain important to you.

Step #4: Consciously recommit yourself to your grand goal.

At the risk of sounding corny, you have to look at the list of grand goals and visions for yourself and say to yourself, "I am capable. I have chosen this for myself. I am going to do this." I'm just giving you those phrases as starting points. Feel free to come up with your version. What's important here is that you consciously commit to these.

Please understand that it takes years to achieve these. It takes quite a bit of sacrifice. But the good news is, by being as conscious of these as possible, you burn them into your mind. It becomes part of your daily ritual when you write and rewrite, and crumple up the goal list. Eventually, it becomes part of you.

Step #5: Take action on your goals.

When you're crushing your daily list of tasks, always remember how they relate to your goals. Then, give yourself some affirmations regarding what you achieved and how they helped you get one step closer to your goal.

This enables you to overcome procrastination. This also pushes you to do your very best in achieving your goals.

This step also makes sure that your goals are at the top of your mind. They are not some distant fantasy or notion that would be nice if it happened. Instead, it becomes immediate.

Food For Thought! #6

"If you always put limits on everything you do, Physical or anything else. It will spread into your work and into your life. There are no limits. There are only plateaus, and you must not stay there, you must go beyond them." -Bruce Lee

_____

_____

_____

_____

_____

_____

_____

_____

_____

_____

_____

_____

_____

_____

_____

_____

_____

And we know that all things work together for good to them that love God, to them who are the called according to his purpose. Romans 8:28 KJV.

"Keep your face to the sunshine, and you cannot see a shadow." Don't' look back; you are not going in that direction. Once you replace negative thoughts with positives ones, you will start having positive thinking, and a willing attitude will allow you to do everything better and enjoy the journey."
-Demetra L. Warrior

_____

_____

_____

_____

_____

_____

_____

_____

And we know that all things work together for good to them that love God, to them who are the called according to his purpose. Romans 8:28 KJV.

"Keep your face to the sunshine, and you cannot see a shadow." Don't' look back; you are not going in that direction. Once you replace negative thoughts with positives ones, you will start having positive thinking, and a willing attitude will allow you to do everything better and enjoy the journey."
-Demetra L. Warrior

Food For Thought! #7

"If you cannot be a poet, be the poem."

What Will You Hope To Be Written About You?

_____

_____

_____

_____

_____

_____

_____

_____

_____

_____

Food For Thought! #8

Persistence Can Change Failure into Extraordinary Achievements!

Is what you are doing bringing joy, love, or purpose?

_____

_____

_____

_____

_____

_____

_____

_____

_____

_____

Food For Thought! #9

"The difference between a warrior and ordinary man is that a warrior sees everything as a challenge, while ordinary man sees everything as either a blessing or a curse."

_____

_____

_____

_____

_____

_____

_____

_____

_____

_____

_____

Food For Thought! #10

"A black belt is nothing more than a belt that goes around your waist. Being a black belt is a state of mind and attitude.

_____

_____

_____

_____

_____

_____

_____

_____

_____

_____

Living Your Purpose

"No matter how you may excel in the art of Karate and your scholastic endeavors, nothing is more important than your behavior and your humanity as observed in daily life."

We know that life is best lived on purpose. Like everything else in the universe, life begins with God. Whether we realize it or not, God has a plan for our lives, and it starts with a divine calling, a direction in which he is leading us.

When we welcome God into our hearts and establish a genuine relationship with him, he will begin, in time, to make his purposes known.

Sometimes God's intentions are clear to us; other times, his plans appear hazy at best. But even on those difficult days when we're not sure which way to turn, we must never lose sight of these overriding facts: God created us for a reason; He has important work for us to do; and He's waiting patiently for us to do it.

We must keep in mind that the Bible says, "And we know that all things work together for good for those who love God, for those who are called according to his purpose." Romans 8:28

What Do You Feel Your Purpose In Life Is?

_____

_____

_____

_____

_____

_____

_____

_____

_____

_____

_____

_____

How do you measure yourself?

"If size mattered, the elephant would be king of the jungle."

_____

_____

_____

_____

_____

_____

_____

_____

_____

_____

Is What You Are Doing Bringing Joy, Love, Or Purpose?

_____

_____

_____

_____

_____

_____

_____

_____

_____

_____

_____

_____

What Are You Putting Your Time And Energy Into Most?

_____

_____

_____

_____

_____

_____

_____

_____

_____

_____

_____

Is There A Mountain In Your Life That You Need To Climb?

_____

_____

_____

_____

_____

_____

_____

_____

_____

_____

_____

_____

_____

Spirit, Body And Soul!

"Beloved, I wish above all things that thou mayest prosper and be in health, even as thy soul prospered." 3 John 1:2 KJV.

We know how important it is to feed our bodies with nourishing foods and get plenty of exercise and rest. Such actions help our bodies to be as healthy as they were created to be and to perform at their peak condition. You must remember that you may have a small body, but great strength. You may have an ordinary mind, but great wisdom. You may have a wounded heart, but great courage. You may have a weary soul, but great love.

And one must remember that it is also important to feed our souls with the kind of nourishment we need to maintain a healthy balance between our spirit, soul, and body. We must feed our souls with divine ideas that stimulate creative actions by spending time in prayer with God.

Just remember that your own mind is a weapon. Your heart is an asset. Your soul is a treasure. Your life is a jewel.

In prayer, we give thanks for the marvelous abilities of our body and for the smooth and efficient way it functions. We are also grateful for the spiritual nourishment we receive during this sacred time with God.

Blessed by God, we must truly express our appreciation: *"Thank you, God, for nourishing our souls! And remember, also, that the mind is its own consciousness, the heart is its own emotions, and the soul is its own eternity."* -Khalid Masood

Have You Checked Your Health Today?

_____

_____

_____

_____

_____

_____

_____

_____

_____

_____

_____

_____

_____

Food For Thought! #11

"A black belt is nothing more than a belt, a piece of cloth. Your goal should not be to get your black belt. Your goal should be to be a black belt. Being a black belt is a state of mind, a way of life."

"Relativity is a beautiful, irrefutable truth." -Black Belt Quote.com

_____

_____

_____

_____

_____

_____

_____

Don't worry! Try to be happy!

Bipolar Disorder

This is a part of many people's lives that many do not wish to talk about, but I truly believe that the more we know, the more we can grow and help others who may be worse off in our shoes. Bipolar Disorder is a severe mental illness characterized by extreme mood swings.

They can include extreme excitement episodes or extreme depressive feelings. But when understood, one can see the beginning of this severe disorder developing. Little do people know that it is a widespread (more than 3 million cases per year in the US) mental illness.

Please understand that this illness, like many others, is treatable by a medical professional and it will take time and can sometimes last for several years or be a lifelong affair.

Affected individuals experience episodes of depression and episodes of mania. Bipolar disorder lasts for a lifetime, with treatments aiming at managing the symptoms through psychotherapy and medication.

When I was younger, I noticed that I would be very happy and maybe a bad memory would happen to me. Then I would fall to an all-time low. My symptoms last for a few days or a couple of weeks and sometimes last for up to a month.

The symptoms vary during the manic and depressive phases. And without any symptoms, in between episodes of mania and depression. The manic phase is characterized by extreme happiness, hopefulness, and excitement, irritability, anger, fits of rage and hostile behavior, restlessness, agitation, rapid speech, poor concentration and judgment, increased energy, less need for sleep, unusually high sex drive, setting unrealistic goals and paranoia.

Then there's the depressive phase, which includes sadness and crying and feelings of hopelessness, worthlessness, and guilt. This phase often brings back many of your life's failures times ten, and you will begin to feel like the world is against you and nothing that you have already accomplished will matter.

The other part is that you will lose energy, lose interest or pleasure in everyday activities, and have difficulty concentrating and making decisions. This will result in irritability as a result of the need for more sleep or sleeplessness. You will often not even notice that you have a change in appetite and that your weight loss/gain has kicked in.

One must remember that worrying is like a rocking chair. It gives you something to do, but it gets you nowhere. Glenn Turner's formal name is Glenn Turner.

Many times, for me, I feel that the best thing for me to do is to put on dark clothes and stand on the railroad tracks and end it all. But, unfortunately, there are times when suicidal thoughts and attempts at suicide try to take hold. But if only you can just make it through the next minute, then the next hour, strive to make it through that entire day, and hope for a better tomorrow.

My biggest challenge was admitting that I had a problem, followed by going to the doctor's office and sitting down to talk with them. Then one will understand that bipolar disorder lasts for a lifetime, with treatments aiming at managing the symptoms through psychotherapy and medication.

We must understand that mood stabilizers are available to assist you in controlling extreme mood variations. Carbamazepine, Lamotrigine, and Valproate are antipsychotic medications used to treat symptoms of psychosis such as hallucination.

With me writing this book "More Than A Martial Artist", I hope that I will also help others realize that it is OK NOT to be OK. Olanzapine, Quetiapine, Lurasidone and Cetirizine also help.

"The struggles we endure today will be the 'good old days' we laugh about tomorrow." -Aaron Lauritsen

Antidepressants and other medications are just a few examples of medications that can help to stabilize mood swings—Sertraline, Fluoxetine, Citalopram, Desvenlafaxine, Duloxetine, Lev milnacipran, Venlafaxine as well.

Although it takes many trials and a lot of patience while looking and trying the meds to see which best fits you, in the end, all that matters is that you don't give up. There have been times when I have had to climb the mountain twice a day back-to-back, climbing over 3000 steps just to try to get relief from the pain, but in the end, it would give me the comfort that I was looking for.

Anxiolytic drugs are also available to help with anxiety. With proven drugs and expert doctors, if only you take the first step, you can know that, at least, you are on the right track. Alprazolam, Clonazepam, Diazepam, Lorazepam, Oxazepam are some other drugs that the doctor may try to help ease your pain.

Do You Find That It Is Ok Not To Be Ok?

Believe You Can

ROMANS 12:2 KJV *"And be not conformed to this world, but be transformed by the renewing of your mind, that you may prove..."* Romans 12:2 *"And be not conformed to this world, but be transformed by the renewing of your mind, that you may prove what is the good, and acceptable, and perfect, will of God."*

Often, your world can shift without preparation. That is when you have to say, OK, it's time to get my mind right. It can be tempting to throw in the towel.

You might even have walked away from what you really wanted to believe, that maybe this battle was not one you could win.

When you feel like you're on the verge of giving up, you need to keep fighting the good fight against all odds.

You may wish you could take a small break to think through a new strategy, or you may have thought you had already quit for good and now find yourself wanting to get back in the ring again.

Sometimes, walking away is exactly what you need to gain perspective and return to shatter the wall that keeps you from your dreams. You wouldn't be the first person to believe the path you're on is too tough to handle. Sometimes you need to expose some of your weaknesses just to move forward.

Remember, it's a faith walk, but with God guiding you, you'll be fine. Sometimes we lose focus when we get wrapped up in our feelings. It's important to make a goal. Then strategize the action plan. Focus on what you can do rather than what you can't.

Do You Believe You Can?

_____

_____

_____

_____

_____

_____

_____

_____

_____

_____

_____

_____

Remember When

I can do all things through Christ which strengthened me.
Philippians 4:13 KJV-

Remember that these are words that many of us have heard many times before. We like to call them "Flashback Moments". Unfortunately, these are also moments that can be the hardest.

Rather than being about abuse or a problem of some kind, remembering things like abuse can also be about rejection. Because your memory can bring back so many bad things, you must also not forget that there were good things that happened to you as well.

Living with abusive memories can either torment you into depression or cause you to rise and help to help someone else. The first step is to stand up for yourself and acknowledge the abuse that has occurred.

Whether it is physical or mental or sexual, you must deal with it if you want to function with a positive mindset. God wants us to be open-minded to new opportunities, even if they scare us. We can do this through his strength and not our own.

Remembering the past can sometimes define you and hold you back, but you must remember that you are always in control of your emotions. You must remember that you can do all things through him. That gives YOU strength!

What Do You Remember?

Sometimes You Just Gotta Hold Your Head High!

Study to shew thyself approved unto God, a workman that needeth not to be ashamed, rightly dividing the word of truth. 2 Timothy 2:15 KJV

We must learn to go forward with our shoulders back, and our heads held high. We must remember to take some things with a smile. Then, with our spirit and perseverance, we must put our intelligence, passions, and talents into action.

Keeping your head up when life tries to knock you down is one of those skills you cannot have if you want to live a happy and successful life.

Things are never as easy as we would like, and many aspects of life are beyond our control, which is why learning to cope with failure and disappointment is critical for our mental health.

We must learn never to let setbacks excuse us from trying repeatedly. Unfortunately, it often takes several attempts to succeed, and we should never allow negative people to influence or direct our actions.

Always face forward and see your whole life shining bright for you. Remember to use your character, ideas, or activism for the good of this world.

Also, never lose sight of the passion that inspires, guides, and always smiles at you. If you follow your desires, they will lead you to your full potential.

Hold to them, and they will keep you honest, caring, kind, and generous with the finest gifts your heart can give. Always remember it is not a man we are trying to please; it is the God we serve. Remember also that if we are going to have hope, we will have to learn to endure the disappointment.

Life pushes us in many ways, testing our strength and demanding up to get out of our comfort zone. The best thing is that if we maintain hope, we are powerful enough to handle both success and disappointment.

What Love Have You Shown Today?

_____

_____

_____

_____

_____

_____

_____

_____

_____

_____

_____

Food For Thought! #12

"If you always put limits on everything you do, physical or anything else, it will spread into your work and into your life. There are no limits. There are only plateaus, and you must not stay there, you must go beyond them." -Bruce Lee

_____

_____

_____

_____

_____

_____

_____

_____

_____

Food For Thought! #13

"If you cannot be a poet, be the poem".

What will you hope to be written about you?

_____

_____

_____

_____

_____

_____

_____

_____

_____

_____

_____

Persistence Can Change Failure Into Extraordinary Achievements

"The difference between a warrior and ordinary man is that a warrior sees everything as a challenge, while ordinary man sees everything as either a blessing or a curse."

How The MMASC Helped Formed My Martial Arts Career

As fighters, we seem to be constantly striving to improve our abilities, always looking for a new challenge, and the MMASC provided precisely that for me.

The MMASC was founded in 1984 by GM Shanna O'Donnell, GM Jefferson Davis, and SGM Richard Osborn, Sr. The Midwest needed a Sports Karate Circuit that would take care of its members, just like the world circuits.

When the MMASC originally started its tournaments, they only had 26 divisions with Grand Championships for Black Belt divisions. Today we have 110 divisions and 13 Grand Championships, along with 13 Grand Championship Runner-ups. The original goal was to annually award the MMASC National Championships with a plaque for their accomplishments. Thirty-seven years later, the MMASC has awarded members custom hoodies, sparring gears, fighting uniforms, plaques, rings, jackets, triple crown awards, and diamond awards. Not only is the membership awarded championship awards, but the MMASC also gives away a massive number of door prizes at the banquet. The MMASC estimated that it gave away over $35,000 in awards and prizes last year. Every person who attended the banquet left with a door prize. The MMASC has 11 tournaments per year. For the past 37 years, an awards banquet has been held at the end of each season. The banquet is to honor and celebrate the accomplishments of the membership. Plaques are given to every member with their name and their place in each division they competed. For example, those who placed 1st in their division received a Championship Hoodie and a Custom Championship ring.

The MMASC Board of Directors estimates they have given away close to $1,000,000 in awards and prizes since 1984. Our long-term goal is to award $100,000 in scholarships to improve the lives of our youth. The MMASC works in our communities by providing clothes and food for the homeless and those less fortunate. The MMASC hopes to distribute 500,000 pounds of food by 2021.

The MMASC, alone, with Williams Elite Martial Arts School, is all about providing a healthy environment for our future leaders. We are about faith, family, fellowship, and fun. We have a pretty simple motto: Do the right thing one white belt at a time.

The MMASC Board of Directors and promoters have been taking care of business since 1984. I have been a part of the organization for the past eight years and have really met great fighters and honed my martial arts skills.

What Seed Have You Planted For The School History?

_____

_____

_____

_____

_____

_____

_____

_____

_____

_____

_____

In life, nothing can satisfy and please your soul as much as helping others. Not only helping the needy will make a difference in their life, but it would also have a lot of benefits for you as well.

Life is 10% what happens to you and 90% of how you react to it. Are you where you want to be in life right now?

Martial Arts Is Like A Mountain Top

You see the top, and you hike and hike, and you climb up, and you finally reach the peak. But then you realize it was a false summit, but in front of you lies an entire new mountain range!

What Are You Putting Your Time In Mostly?

Locals pitch in to provide toys, socks, meals to area homeless

Santa's helpers were able to purchase and deliver 100 presents to 30 children at a homeless shelter in Colorado Springs and bring a Christmas dinner and presents to an additional two families, just days before Christmas.

Fountain resident John Williams sponsored a fundraiser on Facebook seeking donations for toys to help children in a homeless shelter as part of Come On In, Inc.'s Toys for Tots fundraiser. He and Darla Allgood went live on Facebook showing all the toys they purchased with the donations.

Williams, CEO and founder of Come On In, Inc., and Allgood, Come On In Queen and Pageant Director; members of Williams Elite Martial Arts; Brandi Johnson ,Maria Lobdell; the Garcia family, Christine and Jose and their children Jocelyn and Jahvai; and Tiger Rock Martial Arts representatives all volunteered their time to help with the project.

Allgood said, "Christmas is not the only time to give and serve, you can bless someone all year long. John Williams and I were thrilled to bless these families it's not about us, it's about serving them, bringing light, love and hope, that's what Jesus is light, love and hope. It is our duty to love the unloved help the helpless and bring hope to the hopeless. Be the light in someone's life today and bring them hope!"

Williams said Come On In and Fair Finds Home Décor, 104 N. Tejon in Colorado Springs, also sponsored a Sockittoemsockcampaign, collecting 1,000 pairs of socks to give out to the homeless at a mission on Las Vegas Street and to homeless people walking in the Las Vegas Street area.

Williams has been featured in this newspaper for his championship achievements and teaching Tae Kwon Do. He said his heart is in working with youth and community service work.

A couple days before Christmas Williams walked the streets in the area of Las Vegas St. in Colorado Springs talking to homeless people he met handing them a new pair of socks.

Above, Come On In Queen Darla Allgood with a bunch of socks to give out to homeless people this Christmas as part of the Sockittoemsockcampaign.

At right, John Williams and his son, Malakai, and Come On In Queen Darla Allgood with some of the Toys For Tots purchased from funds raised on Facebook.

SUBMITTED PHOTOS

"Some of the people began crying because I handed them socks. They were so thankful for the socks and that I took the time to stop and talk with them." Williams said some people shared how people often treat them like they don't exist. Williams learned some of the people had been bankers and business people and fell on hard times resulting in becoming homeless.

"You never know when something might happen and you could end up in a similar situation," he added. Socks are the most requested and least donated item in homeless shelters.

Is What You Are Doing Bringing Joy, Love, Or Purpose?

_____

_____

_____

_____

_____

Are You Who They Say You Are?

> # DON'T GET CONFUSED
> ## BETWEEN WHAT PEOPLE SAY YOU ARE AND WHO YOU KNOW YOU ARE.
> *- Oprah*
>
> VeryBestQuotes.com

_____

_____

_____

_____

_____

It's time to cross the line for the good of others!

I've Been Through That!

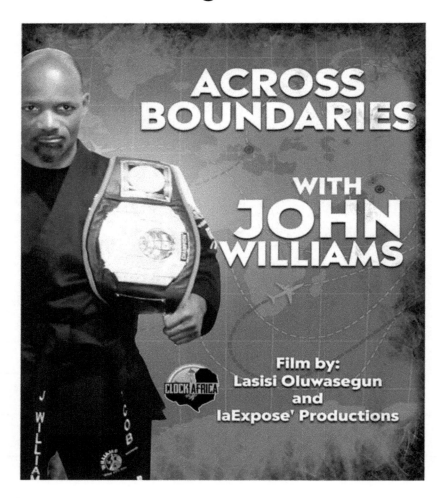

_____

_____

_____

When You Said That I Couldn't!

"Thank You!"

Fighting Tiger Karate School

How do you measure yourself?

_____

_____

_____

_____

_____

_____

_____

_____

_____

_____

_____

_____

Conclusion

Nothing will happen in your life until you take action self-discipline is the key.

Self-discipline is a vital life skill, and it is crucial to any success. If you were to pick 3 top traits that will help ensure your success, self-discipline is one of them. Another one is grit or determination.

The truth is, you can get that amazing life you have dreamed all your life for through self-discipline. You don't necessarily have to be the sharpest tool in the shed. You don't have to be born with a Ph.D. You don't have to be a rock star coming in through the door. But, with enough self-discipline, you will learn what you need to learn to do what you need to do for however long it takes to achieve the big things. The best part about self-discipline is you get a big picture view of the process.

It humbles you. It doesn't turn you to some sort of prima donna who is continuously hungry for attention. This enables you to start looking at life as a series of techniques. Instead of seeing it as a series of humiliations that beat the life out of you, you start seeing life as a series of tests that bring out the best in you.

Far from a scary fire that consumes people and produces excruciating pain, purifying fire refines people just as fire refines gold. When gold is passed through the fire, it becomes pure, it becomes bright and its value shines out.

This is the process of discipline. It's not painless by any stretch of the imagination. But it is necessary pain.

I wish you nothing but the greatest success.

Lightning Source UK Ltd.
Milton Keynes UK
UKHW021006270721
387842UK00014B/1409